William Wales

The Tour of Prince Eblis; His Rounds in Society, Church and State

William Wales

The Tour of Prince Eblis; His Rounds in Society, Church and State

ISBN/EAN: 9783337170998

Printed in Europe, USA, Canada, Australia, Japan

Cover: Foto ©ninafisch / pixelio.de

More available books at **www.hansebooks.com**

THE TOUR

OF

PRINCE EBLIS;

HIS ROUNDS

IN

SOCIETY, CHURCH AND STATE.

CHICAGO:
THE CENTRAL PUBLISHING COMPANY,
1879.

COPYRIGHT SECURED, ACCORDING TO ACT OF CONGRESS.

"Do thou but thy best, and then thou mayst defy the Devil to do his worst."

PREFACE.

There is nothing bad, or anything intended to be even irreverent in this piece; but it is intended to hit hard, absurdities in Fashion, Phariseeism, Morals, Taste, Pretension and sundry other things; and thus do something, possibly, to correct some of the follies of the times.

INDEX.

CHAPTER I.

An Accidental Visitor — Greed Exemplified — Uses of an "Ulster"— Phariseeism—One of the Dens of the Great City—A Convert to "Darwinism." - - - 11–20

CHAPTER II.

The Devil's "Turn Out"—The Devil at a "Charity Ball"— Heroes and Heroines in Opera—"Whipping the Devil 'round the Stump"—Privileged Passengers—"Where is thy Brother?"—A Home for Horses—Fashion's Mouth-Piece. - - - - - - - - - - 23–33

CHAPTER III.

Fashion as a Tantalizer—A glance at the Drama—Opera Bouffe—Wall Street Doings—Pious Uses of Gambling— The Devil in Small Matters—A Walk in Broadway— Effects of "Busting"—Law and its Dealings—Hornets and Flies. - - - - - - - 34–47

CHAPTER IV.

The Bed of Procrustes—Eblis and the Shark—An Old Definition of Patriotism—The Question of a Hell—Fate and Fortune—Blunders of the Human Race—The Sage of Athens and Man of Uz. - - - - - - 48-54

CHAPTER V.

Lies and their Variety—Trapping for Souls—Truth, Savage and Civilized—Honesty, Barbarian and Christian. - 55-63

CHAPTER VI.

A Broadway Procession—Want and its Avengers—"The Devil to Pay"—The Prince at the Capital—Windmills —The Ins and the Outs—The Statue, its Significance— The Monument. - - - - - - - - 64-71

CHAPTER VII.

The True "Third Estate"—The Prince a Lobbyist—Overreached—Mushroom Aristocracy—Secretary Subsidy's Levee—Jenkins on the same—"Rings" and their import. 72-84

CHAPTER VIII.

A Trip to the Provinces—Bidding for Souls—A Learned Professor—The Thirst for Glory—The Soldier's Horoscope— The Young Girl—Pride versus Love—The Miser. - 85-96

CHAPTER IX.

Vessels to Honor and Dishonor—Eblis as an Angler—Fly Fishing and its Victims—Capture of an "Interviewer"—New Locations for Shooting Galleries.   -   -   99–106

CHAPTER X.

Agrarianism—The Red Flag—Beer or Blood—The Meaning of a "Divide"—The Tramps—"The Man with the Poker"—Earthly Hells.   -   -   -   -   -   107–113

CHAPTER XI.

The Prince at the "Hub"—Some Hub Peculiarities—The Puritans and their Theology—Jack and the Parson—Unity and its Difficulties—"Holding the Fort"—Impudence of an Imp—A Stimulant to Patriotism.   -   114–124

CHAPTER XII.

A College Fungus—A "Base" Infliction—Periodical Departures Celestialwards—Clams and Contrition—Celestial Ferry Tickets—Experiences of Job and Moses—Finale. 127–140

LIST OF ILLUSTRATIONS.

	PAGE.
An Accidental Visitor,	13
Phariseeism,	17
A Convert to "Darwinism,"	21
The Devil at a "Charity Ball,"	27
A Home for Horses,	31
Fashion as a Tantalizer,	35
A Glance at the Drama,	39
Wall Street Doings,	43
Honesty—Barbarian and Christian,	61
The Prince at the Capital,	69
Overreached,	73
Mushroom Aristocracy,	77
Secretary Subsidy's Reception,	81
The Soldier's Horoscope,	89
Pride versus Love,	93
The Miser,	97
The "Interviewer,"	103
The Prince at the "Hub,"	115
Hub Theology,	119
A College Fungus,	125
A "Base" Infliction,	129
Clams and Contrition,	133
Pagan Christianity,	137
Finale.	141

THE TOUR OF PRINCE EBLIS.

CHAPTER I.

An Accidental Visitor—Greed Exemplified—Uses of an "Ulster"—Phariseeism—One of the Dens of the Great City—A Convert to "Darwinism."

A youthful Satan on a jaunt one day,
   Around the verge of the Infernal world,
The haunt of such, got in some sort of fray,
   And from its battlements was swiftly hurled;
At first he was disposed to loudly murmur,
But 'lighting in Broadway he liked Terra Firma.

In costume scant, as wrench'd from world Infernal,
   He, in his 'stress, at what seem'd "solid" grasped,
And with wise instinct, as with grip eternal,
   That lump of gold held on to hard and fast:
A sharp young imp, he soon saw all was right,
As Mammon's show-fronts flashed upon his sight.

"The Devil amongst the tailors" was no harm;
  So in he walk'd to one of Fashion's haunts,
And though his tail was wrapp'd around his arm,
  The master-fashioner gave no look askance;
For didn't he see right there before his eyes,
That talisman, GOLD, the first beneath the skies?

And didn't he then and there condone his fears
  At hope of some share of the glittering prize,
And handle carefully that tail as his shears
  Cut here and there to hide it from all eyes?
'Till the young imp, pleased at such kind attention,
Was fain to grin and nod his condescension.

The devil was clad, the fashioner paid, and now,
  The imp would look around to see what's what!
Was warmly clad for one of his kind, for lo!
  A devilish "ulster" girded him about;
'Twas ultra in its length, for walking around,
The infernal garment dragged upon the ground.

So ultra that one day as on he loitered,
  Among some dandies, he 'cognized as one,
—For by this time in Upper Tendom quartered,
  He had become a leader of the ton—
His tail, which dropp'd his trowser's leg below,
The friendly Pat-coat hid from each one's view.

AN ACCIDENTAL VISITOR.

I mention this, because I have a reason
    For being definite in this my rhyme;
The devil had landed rather out of season
    For one who came from such a tropic clime;
But being a visitor to us, *nolens volens*,
He did the best he could wrapp'd up in woolens.

Reflection came, he saunter'd days and nights
    In the world's marts, though partial to Broadway,
For there he saw so many kindred sights,
    That his transition seem'd not much astray;
On every side he saw such assimilation,
He 'gan to conjure plans of annexation.

Not like the process on that beauteous Rhine,
    By war, which came so near a nation squelching,
His sire had plann'd the loss o' Alsace and Lorraine,
    In grief and carnage, whilst hell seem'd a belching;
But here was a world almost, which to annex,
He was quite sure would few of its denizens vex.

He'd look into it straightway, that he would;
    He'd shrewdly notice what was going ahead,
He might find many reasons why he should
    Get such a province for his sharp old dad;
To be sure this region didn't stand alone,
He'd look at all to see what could be done.

As these reflections came upon the rogue
  One winter's morn—'twas Sunday by the way—
He wandered forth to see the styles in vogue
  Of those who in God's temples sing or pray,
Or patronize the pastor;—wrapp'd in's ulster close,
It must be owned he felt somewhat morose.

For why?—the wind 'most took him from his feet,
  In sweeps, as wildly up the street it rose;
The snow too came in swirls, and then some sleet,
  Hit like small shot against his Roman nose;
The imp was roused, he pushed through sleet and snow,
To pause at length, 'neath spire and portico.

And there he saw a sight to please the devil—
  Saw noble steeds close "clipp'd" prance to the gate,
Saw other sights to please the Author of Evil;
  Saw fashion's votaries, furr'd and shawl'd, elate,
Rustle their silks and satins as they greeted
Friends and acquaintances in each fine pew seated;

For warmth and music waited on them there,
  * And soft words, telling of some glorious sphere,
Where fields were always green, a world so fair
  With all that's beautiful, that sigh, nor tear,
Nor vain regret, nor suffering could be known,
That Land of Promise, too, should be their own.

PHARISEEISM.

The imp, he heard all this and laughed in scorn;
  Laugh'd silently, for had the sexton known it,
He would have had him off to prison borne,
  And left in limbo 'till his sin he'd own it;
For why? outside the devil had seen a sight,
To make all imps and demons laugh outright.

There stood the horses, shorn and shivering, teaching
  Lessons of patience to that church unknown;
There froze the coachmen, silently, hours preaching
  Sermons on fortitude to hearts of stone:
Left in the lurch on that high road to bliss,
Consoled to know their masters couldn't it miss.

He thought he'd seen enough for that one day,
  So turn'd towards his smoking-room once more,
But misery! he seem'd to lose his way
  Bewilder'd in the sleet and storm's uproar;
He staggered onward towards a hell on earth,
Where all of evil seem'd to have its birth.

He'd blunder'd down a cross-street as the sound
  Of the great organ still rang in his ears,
A roll of chariot wheels which shook the ground,
  Signalling the scattering of those worshippers,
To palace splendors, wines and viands rare,
Where they "thank'd God they weren't as others are."

The organ sounded peal on peal as yet,
  'Companied close by by peals of maniac laughter;
With these came groans and curses from a set
  Of hideous wretches mad with long disaster;
The devil in's ulster slipp'd in full of glee,
To pass for Patrick fresh from 'cross the sea.

He look'd about him in that awful den
  Of misery and pain, reflex of the fell pit,
No thanking God they weren't as other men,
  For they were wrecks, and well they all knew it;
All they believed in, all they sought for there,
Was brief forgetfulness to drown despair.

The devil at "home," he smiled as at him stared,
  Eyes, bloodshot, through an atmosphere of hell,
Imbibed some "lightning," then rose up quite scared,—
  Something was wrong, just what he could not tell;
Suddenly he vanished in a sulphurous glare,
That whiskey'd burnt his tail off close to the chair.

A CONVERT TO DARWINISM.

CHAPTER II.

The Devil's "Turn Out"—The Devil at a "Charity Ball"—Heroes and Heroines in Opera—"Whipping the Devil around the stump"—Privileged Passengers—"Where is thy Brother?"—A Home for Horses—Fashion's Mouth-Piece.

The imp's mishap was not of Chinese fashion,
   Where loss of tail is loss of standing too,
For though he fled in such a devilish passion,
   He, on reflection, ceased to feel so blue;
He shortened up his ulster on the occasion,
Resolved on a new tour of observation.

Shying the haunts so much like his old home,
   Where other mishaps he might have to mourn,
He turned his face once more toward Upper Tendom,
   To see how Fashion's burdens could be borne;
He'd felt some *ennui* up amongst the grand,
And doubted whether e'en imps such woe could stand.

His "turn out," quite immaculate, I must mention,
  Because his "bits of blood" were from the stables,
Of that great financier who paid attention
  To "watering stock," until the wildest fables
Of Crœsus and his wealth, howe'er displayed,
Were by this "operator" quite thrown in the shade.

This "stock," well fed, not "water'd," show'd their heels
  To all who ventured with them to compete;
Minutes were seconds as the dancing wheels
  Raised dust Olympic all along the street;
The devil's cab was blue picked out with gold,
And all eyes followed it as on it rolled.

Where'er it stopped the doors flew open wide;
  At boudoir windows how the laces fluttered!
And as his Highness slowly made his stride
  Up marble steps, how awe-struck flunkies stuttered!
Not Duke Alexis or proud Albion's heir,
So made the habitues of Fifth Avenue stare.

The devil was pleased; was flattered, past all doubt:
  And next—what seem'd a movement rather funny,
Got up a ball to bring the ton right out,
  To dance for "Charity" in getting money;
Of course he laughed and chuckled to himself,
As waltz and polka brought some trifling pelf.

To be sure, some few were fain to stay at home,
  They couldn't dance to any sinful "scraping,"
The violin as "fiddle" made them sigh and groan,
  At human wickedness all bad things aping;
These compromised with Conscience by a dance
To the "piano," as their only chance.

'Twas at this "Charity" the Prince came near exposure,
  In these "round dances," being such a dancer;
Indeed his pedigree came near disclosure,
  Because in "polking" he was so fine a prancer;
He drew all eyes—all but "bewitched" the girls,
As pantingly they kept up with his whirls.

Like teetotums all spun to music's sound,
  Some elders trying vainly to look pleased,
And if young waists seem'd clasp'd too close around:
  "How could one keep up unless tightly squeezed?"
A small hand too press'd on each brawny shoulder;
What pleasanter sight to each mamma beholder.

As India-rubber the Prince seem'd lithe and strong,
  Eliciting the envy of his "set,"
Until, at last, one lisping Freddy Long,
  Declared aloud,—"he beath the devil, you bet!"
The Prince surprised, delighted at such mention,
Blurted right out,—"*they're all my dad's invention!*" *

    * See Appendix, Note A.

Luckily for him, they laid this to champagne,"
Their wits by this time getting somewhat frisky,
Not more, because all gentlemen refrain,
From getting stupid as louts do on whiskey;
So it passed off, causing no marked attraction,
The Prince having charmed them by his "grace and action."

And then the girls; the girls! the girls!! the girls!!!
It didn't stop there—they couldn't talk enough,
Of one "so charming!"—"were there other worlds
To give more pleasure?"—"He was not a muff!"*
"Indeed!" exclaimed Miss Florence Jane Amour,
"He really lifted *me* quite off the floor!"

The devil liked opera, 'specially such as brought
To mind the doings of his followers here and there;
Lucrezia Borgia was a favorite sought,
With Don Giovanni of morals rare:
But tired of these with constant repetitions,
His fashionable friends shared with him these conditions.

So in the church where once a week they met,
They "whipped the devil around the stump," he heard,
With organ music, solo and quartette,
To whet the senses of great Fashion's herd;
The devil soon found his choicest warblers there,
Leading these operas with anxious care.

* See Note B.

THE DEVIL AT A CHARITY BALL.

Meanwhile, the tens of thousands!—what did they—
   The' world outside, without a sign of seating,
Within such walls?—what chance to sing or pray,
   To—as the Puritans put it—"go to meeting!"
Were these vast palace-cars for God to approve,
When but the rich were ticketed above?*

The devil pondered, noting each rich feature,
   The meaning of such wealth displayed within,
And at the portal, jostled by the preacher,
   He asked: "Is this a Hospital for Sin?" †
"What heathen asks such questions? 'Tis for praise!
For blessings given us in unnumbered ways."

"I thought as much!" the devil soliloquized,
   Then turned on's heel with grim Satanic smile,
To think that men could yield what most they prized,
   Their gold, themselves to foolishly beguile;
"Where is thy brother?"—thought ne'er to them given,
As up they sent that steeple towards high heaven.

The devil was posed; he sauntered forth once more,
   Scanning the buildings with a slow precision,
And soon he stood another church before,
   A "home for horses!"—could he trust his vision?
There were its pillars, date, its front of stone,
Its carvings desecrate, its beauty gone.

      * See Note C.   † See Note D.

And looking further, coming into view,
  Were other structures reared to the Most High,
In all ways desecrate, as all did show
  Some sign of degradation plain to the eye;
Mammon and Bacchus, Thespis,—all were there,
To shame the builders of those temples fair.

*   *   *   *   *   *   *   *   *

Up to this time, young Eblis had encounter'd
  The mere extremes of what was round him there,
Had stumbled on them as he careless saunter'd,
  Through the metropolis with easy air;
But now he thought on business to proceed,
Since some report his keen old sire might need.

But here he found the "Court End" fairly loaded,
  With rank absurdities based on grand assumption;
Absurdities in the Old World long ago exploded,
  The authors "laughed dead" as without any gumption;
A job anew to explode them being so great,
As worse, by far, than "blowing up Hell Gate."

The wantonness of wealth, what power can measure?
  One Gotham exquisite with more dimes than brains,
In imitation of an English dolt, at leisure,
  Gets up a "stage-coach" with infinite pains;
And condescending on it to act the driver,
He "tips his hat" for any dirty stiver.

A HOME FOR HORSES.

One journal keeps a "Court List" for the *ton*,
   Tells weekly what is doing at balls and parties,
At "Kettle Drums," "receptions," and so on,
   At "conversations" who were the chief smarties;
Does the man-milliner for each rich parvenu,
For Shoddy and Petroleum raised in calico.

In all these matters Gotham is the model,
   The "Glass of Fashion and the mould of form;"
And whoso dares to take it in his noddle,
   To question this of course must raise a storm;
A "tempest in a tea pot," after all,
For fashion—a female, being hit, will squall.

CHAPTER III.

Fashion as a Tantalizer—A Glance at the Drama—Opera Bouffe—Wall Street Doings—Pious Uses of Gambling—The Devil in Small Matters—A Walk in Broadway—Effects of "Busting"—Law and its Dealings—"Hornets and Flies."

Eblis had seen the fashions, dresses quite "decolleté,"
  "Pullbacks,"* as well as other o'er shrewd inventions,
To spur the spoonies in their hours of jollity,
  Over champagne, to "definite attentions;"
And next he thought he'd look in on the Drama,
To see what it presented any lamer.

The first sight that he saw was the "Black Crook;"
  Young Eblis blushed as on that phalanx strode,
And then his sides with mirth so strongly shook,
  A fat dame near, surprise and anger showed;
He saw that as an Agency of Evil,
This get up well might "shame the very devil!"

* See Note E.

FASHION AS A TANTALIZER.

He asked the lady—" What all this could mean?
And hoped she'd please to pardon the intrusion;
He was a stranger there and rather green,
Would she explain what brought to him confusion?"
With patronizing smile and broad vernacular,
She said "'twas jolly and was term'd spectac-er-ler."

"Spectacular indeed!"—young Eblis queried—
" A spectacle all *limbs*, or nearly so,
For it is plain that blue and red lights varied,
Take nothing from that feature of the show!"
"Get out!"—the lady cried—in wrath once more,
She'd "raised the devil!" for he fled for the door.

It took cool air as he went up Broadway,
To quite compose him for another glance
At aught like that; but happening on Aimeé,
He saw enough of that sweet school of France;
A devil confounded! brought to such a state,
He would retire and try to recuperate.

* * * * * * * * * *
The devil had quite regained his equipoise,
So in on Wall street thought he'd take a look;
Perhaps might learn a thing or two 'midst noise
'Bout "shorts" and "margins," just like other folk;
Was somewhat curious too 'bout "bull" and "bear,"
Though strongly urged of such beasts to beware.

There happened on that day to be a "corner,"
   And sundry "breaks" and "rallies" by each "ring;"
But "hell broke loose" could hardly match each "goner,"
When these as "bulls," for "bears" went bellowing;
And when the row broke up for want of "rocks,"
Ruin met a host of gamblers in stocks.

Some were "lame ducks," some crept "beneath a cloud;"
   One hung himself to make his losses good;
But when the smoke had clear'd and that fierce crowd
   Of Mammon worshippers had understood,
They'd lost on "rumors" sent forth as a snare,
It seem'd "legitimate," though false as fair.

No one lost caste by what he said or did,
   Unless his crime was being short of cash!
For though they stood on nothing and had bid,
   For thousands in a way so desperate, rash,
And lost or won without a maravedi,
'Twas but a matter of course with the most needy.

One pious gambler, howe'er, I should note,
   Would show his thankfulness for his rich plunder;
He didn't "buy candles for the saints," but wrote,
   Giving a college thousands!—'twas a blunder!
Before they got the pious offering, he "busted,"
To the great grief of the "Profs." who in gambling trusted.

A GLANCE AT THE DRAMA.

'Twas hard to be so "spoiled by the Egyptians"
  They thought, instead of getting " spoils"—and then,
Under " the chastening of these sore afflictions,"
  They thought of "Daniel in the lions' den!"
It was to them, in truth, a " bitter cup!"
Their Daniel stay'd 'till " regularly chaw'd up!"

His rival " operator" on this score him got
  —As in all else—in planting the Tree of Knowledge,
For with part proceeds of his " Watering Pot,"
  He founded solidly i' the South a famous college;
And canonized almost for that same act,
It stands a monument of superior " tact."

Enough of Wall street, Eblis was amazed,
  To find that paper promises and brags,
Could work such wonders,—fact, was almost dazed,
  To learn that gold could rival find in rags;
He 'gan to think that Wall street " beat Old Nick,"
In conjuring devilment by " going on tick."

All this, of course, to Eblis gave great pleasure,
  It was refreshing quite and he'd report it;
His sire would be delighted when he'd leisure,
  To look into it as he'd fully note it;
And then in cheating, Wall street wasn't alone,
He would look further on amongst his own.

He'd see the traffickers in other callings;
  Would see what sordid Gain could do elsewhere;
How Greed and Cant could stand each other's maul-
    ings,
  The field to work was rich beyond compare;
In fact, 'twas time to much extend his sphere,
If he'd improve the chance of his visit here.

He'd see some smaller Wall street where temptation
  Didn't strive the conscience thus to tear and rend;
Would learn if anywhere in all Creation,
  There was much conscience where gain was the end;
And passing Fulton Market with this thought,
He stopp'd forthwith—here was the chance he sought.

Right by his side a fruit-stall spread its treasures,
  Rich with the products of all lands and climes;
The smaller fruits displayed in tiny measures,
  In pyramidal heaps the larger kinds;
Of these, the apples were by far most plenty,
The dealer a nice girl, perhaps near twenty.

Simple she seem'd as modestly her look,
  Responded to a lady visitor's soft tone;
Her face so fair that one could hardly brook,
  That in her bosom guile was ever known;
"Apples," the lady called for, and her hand
Sought a small pyramid upon the stand.

WALL STREET DOINGS.

The devil soon saw in that nice pile a cheat!
  It was a stack of pippins hard and small,
Yet thatched all over with a roof quite neat,
  Of better fruit to make this pass for all;
The white hand 'gan to dig beneath the pile,
The lady watching it silently meanwhile.

The devil could scarcely credit his own eyes,
  The fruit was heap'd anew so trim and well;
So fair to the sight that great was his surprise,
  To find the quiet customer rebel:
"I shall not take your apples, you're a fraud!"
The girl not wincing at a charge so broad.

As Eblis look'd around, 'twas all the same;
  E'en children seem'd well taught in the same school,
And quite unconscious that a jot of blame,
  Attached to acts their patrons to befool,—
The apple dealer feeling no remorse,
  Had borne the lady's charge as a matter of course!

So back on Broadway Eblis roved again,
  Past plate-glass windows rich with shawls and laces,
The street a panorama filled amain,
  With brilliant equipages and pretty faces;
Where lusty manhood paced its little hour
Of bliss, to stumble and be seen no more.

But what anew surprised him,—nay, astounded!
　　Even in times so stringent as of late,
A something which all old ideas confounded,
　　Of profit on investments at some rate—
The world of merchandise seem'd up "for cost,"
And "less" than that—such was each vendor's boast.

And when one "bursted," bankrupted, "went under,"
　　And simple souls began to feel some pity
The chiefest evidence of loss of plunder,
　　Was some new equipage to stun the city;
Perhaps an opera-box for the next season,
A yacht, or trifles like these—"all in reason!"

The devil was puzzled quite with what he saw
　　In these extremes of Gothamite society;
And if he scann'd that complication—law,
　　He found amusement even to satiety;
On all sides "catching flies" 'twas plain to see,
It let "the hornets" mostly go quite "free!"

'Twas "compromise," for instance, with those public robbers,
　　Who, "brought to grief," could only part disgorge;
The Judges of the Courts e'en turning jobbers,
　　In felony to let thieves run at large;
"Plate sin with gold"—of course all know the rest,
So oft illustrated as to make it a test.

Some bolder rogues, of law in utter scorn,
   A bank would rob, grab thousands at a dash,
And when the startled losers the next morn
   Went almost mad at their great loss of cash,—
The Police summon'd, they with looks quite wise,
Would straight suggest, with the rogues a " compro-
   mise."

Say half a million had been stolen thus,
   The style o' the job showing whose skill was task'd,
"All could be had safe back without any fuss,
   For, say, one-third, and the pledge—no questions
   ask'd ;"
Perhaps a month would hardly pass away
When the thieves' " turn out " would amaze Broadway.

And this going on, whilst day by day " the law "
   Would seize on wretches for some petty crime,
Perhaps for stealing an old axe, or saw,
   A hat, or shoes, or stale loaf worth a dime;
And then what righteous indignation shone,
As justice immured him in its walls of stone.

CHAPTER IV.

The Bed of Procrustes—Eblis and the Shark—An Old Definition of Patriotism—The Question of a Hell—Fate and Fortune—Blunders of the Human Race—The Sage of Athens and Man of Uz.

The next thing seen by Eblis was a "Strike;"*
  Because, since Eden, sweat's been drawn too freely,
But in the wish that all should fare alike,
  Their mode seem'd a Procrustean measure really;
"Eight hours per day, and pay at equal rates,"
Of course makes even, "light" and "heavy weights."

A "botch," or shirk, being thus far "short" was "stretched;"
  A "skill'd' thus "taller" cut off very short;
The lazy and industrious would have fetched,
  The same wage thus when tried at labor's mart;
And more—no single one must work at all,
No matter if starvation was the thrall!

*See Note F.

So much impossible,—yet thousands strove,
  To make a fight upon that basis pay;
And seeking sympathy through the streets they rove,
  Their banners bravely flouting the dull day;
Alack! how coldly turns the world aside,
As onward flows that vast tumultuous tide.

Poor fellows!—e'en the devil felt their case,
  The sport of circumstances they couldn't control;
What strong prerogatives has Wealth in the race,
  For careless comfort, that great earthly goal:
How "luck" beguiles as men strive for't in vain,
One of life's hardest problems to explain.

Then there's the "sharks!" par excellence the sharks!
  The dry old skinflints known as "Cent per Cents;"
Who prey on misery and from whom all sparks,
  Of pity have died out in ash and stench;
Young Eblis called on one of these to claim
Relationship, so next announced his name.

"Well, yes; I'm glad to see so true a friend;
  You want some money! well it's hard to get;
I haven't any myself which I can lend,
  But then I know a friend who may it let;
How much must you have? it's very hard to get!"
Parroting these words—" it's very hard to get."

Young Eblis wasn't in want, but "fast and loose,"
   He thought he'd have some fun in "playing" the creature,
For he himself was far from such a goose,
   As not to see the "shark" in every feature:
At last old Gripus brought some dirty "rags,"
Pretending they were from his friend—Mons. Moneybags.

"'Twas hard to get, he must have cent. per cent.:
   I knew your father: yes, I knew your brother;
I could but oblige ye, so my time I've spent,
   To serve one just as I would serve the other;—"
—The imp, in terror, fled from such a moke,
For fear he'd break his sire at one fell stroke.

Of "Patriotism," so much young Eblis heard,
   He felt quite curious one may be sure;
When orators so deeply the populace stirred,
   He thought the inspiration must be pure:
But soon found that as a primary condition,
There might be something in an old definition.

An ancient sage, deep in word meaning lore,
   Was ask'd to state "what Patriotism is?"
Roused by this query put by a constant bore,
   He gave a pithy answer to the quiz:
"Patriotism!"—he roar'd—with voice much like a "groundswell,"
"Patriotism, sir, is the last refuge of a scoundrel!"

That may not be good rhyme, it is good sense,
  Since demagogues so often win high station,
Getting their places by some bald pretense
  Of patriotism to shame us as a nation;
They crawl in slime to points they could not soar,
The m-asses, their partisans, duping o'er and o'er.

One of the marvels of the time, he found,
  Was bold denial of there being a Hell,
Supported by fancies more or less profound,
  Of thousands, self persuaded 'twas a "sell;"
"No rogue," he thought, "e'er felt the halter draw,
Retaining good opinion of the law."

Here he soliloquized—"If the fools could tell,
  How each a part of my domain he carried,
In his own bosom bearing his own hell
  When by its conscience each bad life is harried—
They might approximate what they'll never know,
Until the worst may meet the worst, below."

The cry—"No Hell!" to him was the best thing out!
  The ancient creed had help'd stop emigration:
But with no check upon the downward route,
  No fear of aught when yielding to temptation—
To crime, he'd look now for a large accession,
From those who made of villainy a profession.

As matters stood, the gallows had little terror,
   To any wretch—'twas but the "gate to glory,"
To all who took it, and a mere vulgar error,
   To think that murderers, nathless grim and gory,
Could not, for the time, be made as "white as snow,"
By those whose business 'twas to "put 'em through!"

So some had tried to cheat him of his prey,
   Whilst others denied his "personality" long ago;
And now comes Canon Farrar with his say,
   Denying him his domain in toto;
The queerest thing of all is—not one knows,
A single step that way beyond his nose.

Busy, as proverbially the devil has been,
   In walking "to and fro" the earth all o'er,
To meddle in matters quite beyond our ken,
   Such as to smite "just" Job with boils full sore,
The earth more rife with deviltry these days,
Needs subs of his to post him in its ways.

And so young Eblis found himself again,
   Scanning the doings of our civilization,
Looking around to see if that refrain,
   Chanted so loud, of "progress" is the occasion
For humbug infinite in various guise,
To strike all quiet lookers-on with surprise.

Noting more closely than had been his wont,
  The endless blunders of the human race,
" Blunders" being worse than crimes to bear the brunt
  Of untold suffering in almost every case—
The imp, more charitable than at the beginning,
Found numbers vast "more sinned against than sin-
    ning."

What's Fate? what Fortune? Who so wise can tell?
  Yet these have vassals had from earliest ages;
Most men are victims to some horrid "sell,"
  Even those reputed as earth's greatest sages;
How came the sage of Athens by a dame,
Her name, for her kind, the devil's own synonym?

He said, "to teach him patience!"—what a reason!
  —More an excuse for being badly fooled,—
No man wants prodding in and out of season,
  No matter to what ends he may be schooled;
Job fared no better, for besides his boils,
His wife tormented him when in Satan's toils.

Covered with sores so that he couldn't lie
  Or sit in peace, his stately dame drew near,—
Told him to "Curse his Maker, and then die!"
  Such was the comfort she vouchsafed him there;
The man of Uz, like him of Athens, later,
Could scarce avoid that fate—a "woman hater."

They'd blunder'd:—then those "blunders worse than
  crimes,"
Fruitful of sorrows which can never cease,
Blunders, which to the victim seem at times,
  Worse than "the Shirt of Nessus" to his peace,—
Blunders in Love, in Friendship, even in Hate,
With but Remorse for which to compensate.

That gift of Dejanira's—what a blunder!
  And yet a gift in love, beyond all doubt;
So, who at times is not quite given to wonder,
  How even his best intentions may "pan out;"
"The devil is in it!" is the forced exclamation,
To afford poor blundering mortals consolation.

The Conquerors of the world were ruined by blunders,
  The Macedonian, Roman, Corsican—all,
They took no heed when Fate gave warning thunders,
  But plunged right onward to their final fall;
The devil, of course, misled them o'er and o'er,
As he duped Mother Eve so long before.

CHAPTER V.

Lies and their Variety—Trapping for Souls—Truth, Savage and Civilized—Honesty, Barbarian and Christian.

Of "sins" young Eblis found as dark as night,
    The sin of *lying* marked all "good society,"
Since Christendom beats Heathendom out of sight,
    In every shade and shadow of variety;
For class'd as "peccadillos," and no worse,
Of Christian civilization it seems the curse.

Lies are they of all kinds, of Business; Fashion;
    Lies of Politeness; Wantonness; of Crime;
Sometimes the church, whilst it doth lay the lash on
    All sin, with zeal which reaches the sublime,
Has stucco'd front to cheat each passer-by
With show of stone, to all, of course, a lie.

Those fibs of the elect: those Plymouth dreamings,
　　Avouched by oaths, no stronger ever heard,
The outside world aghast stood at such seemings:
　　Of those who assumed so much to "revere the
　　　　Word;"
Who were the liars, though, will ne'er be known,
'Till that Great Day when each his lies must own.

The business lie, from calicoes to laces,
　　The lie of fashion, that cool "Not at home!"
The lie polite, which, while with smiling faces,
　　Welcoming each visitor as in they come,
In secret, wishes e'en Old Nick might seize 'em,
So that such callers may no longer tease 'em.

In trapping souls, the sharpest scheme of all,
　　To catch the wariest as in a snare,
Deadlier than jungle-corral, or pitfall,
　　Which make the cautious elephant beware—
Is one so glaring that it seems amazing,
That any soul is caught that is worth saving.

The hunter knows that when he traps for beaver,
　　Or mink, or otter, that he is most boggled
When with the oldsters he would play deceiver,—
　　That youthful rodents are most easily gobbled:
In the case in hand the devil has had his way,
Until men—"best and oldest"—are his prey.

For taxes, the law must an "assessment" make;
   That is the trap;—and next must come the "list;"
And next, the assessed his solemn oath must take,
   The value's "correct," e'en though poor conscience twist;
For "custom" sanctions that a wholesale lie,
To show a *part's* the *whole*, may truth defy!

The piano, worth *three* hundred, put at "one;"
   The elegant furniture worth *one thousand*, "four;"
The carriage, *six* hundred, it not long has run,
   Put it at "two," or even somewhat lower;
Fix these and other items so that you
May pay a moiety of what's really due.

Both sides conniving at this formal cheat,
   Participants in what is all untrue,
Ah! what a reckoning myriads must meet
   When all this "shuffling" is brought to view;
Well might the devil, as he scann'd these matters
Regard complacently his hosts of trappers.

So cheap are oaths!—how cheaper still are souls!
   God, from his throne call'd witness to such fraud;
Why, that beats China, as it surely moulds
   A nation to a course of lies so broad;
A soul in the scale weighed 'gainst the grimy dollar,
The heathen world might laugh at cheat so hollow.

A witness on the stand, in case of crime,
   How closely follows all of truth he knows;
Though some poor wretch's life be at the time
   In peril, where his words are cruel blows;
He a "high duty" must perform, and so
Straight to the scaffold dooms the man to go.

But touch his pocket, all the nerves there end,
   Too oftentimes which give him conscious life;
Each God-given faculty subject to it lend
   A furious strength to make all gain, hot strife;
What wonder such forget they have a soul,
Or peril it readily for the paltriest dole.

In short, young Eblis found what in despair,
   A French philosopher called "one grand deception,"
That half the world was bent on making fair
   The false, to cheat the rest beyond conception;
That shams the millions got up too for gold,
Whilst other millions by these shams were sold.

'Twas in this mood that on one pleasant eve,
   Young Eblis dropp'd in on a mission meeting,
Where speeches showed how Christian souls did grieve
   O'er heathen wickedness 'mid sighs and weeping:
Where first one speaker and anon, another,
Implored for aid to convert his heathen brother.

But midst all this young Eblis silent noted
   A venerable and weather-beaten wight,
Who in the outset neither spoke nor voted
   On any scheme that came up on that night;
But listening patiently to each objurgation
On heathen wickedness, begg'd some slight attention.

He said that truthfulness was the great mark,
   The great distinction of a noble nation—
At least it should be—and no stain so dark
   Could lie 'gainst any as e'en mere evasion;
But—grief to say—the heathen were more true,
As, by their leave, he would proceed to show.

At this the Prince cried "Hear! Hear!" English fashion,
   But recollected that would never do;
And soon 'twas proved, for with no little passion,
   The Reverend Chairman looking black and blue,
Came down upon him with an angry greeting,
And threat of "Police" for "disturbing the meeting."

The ancient traveller kept on his narration—
   He said that "sojourning in his younger days,
Upon our frontiers with a tribe or nation
   Of savages, he came to know their ways;
Whilst there, report came of a fight and murder,
At point remote upon that far off border.

"The Government Agent, all alert to arrest
　An absent Chief, suspected at the time,
Started two "runners" at a pace their best,
　To bring him back to answer for the crime:
After some days gone by, they reappear—
'Well! where's the man you chased? why isn't he
　　here?'

"'*He said he didn't do it!*'—so we came,
　To state the fact as from his lips we had it;
Of course, we knew if he had been to blame
　For murder, or aught else, he would have said it;
He would disdain'd his life to save by a lie,
A rule of his tribe as it has been alway!'

"And so it was—the white man stood reproved,
　For that his people couldn't have stood the test,
For when some days elapsed the crime was proved,
　Another chieftain having the crime confest—
The official thought of all the tricks to confuse
The Courts of Law, to save guilt from its dues.

"True were they long ago," the ancient said,
　"Before our people lies as legacies gave:
It's possible that now they are as bad
　As even ourselves, who purpose them to save!
True were they, not unlike another nation,
O'er whom we pride ourselves for our Christianization.

HONESTY, BARBARIAN AND CHRISTIAN.

"It's years a many, since as a castaway
  Of a wreck'd ship I stood upon the shore;
Amongst some Turks who'd dragg'd us from the spray
  And surf to give us life and strength once more;
And having saved some lading for us besides,
Had piled it on the beach beyond the tides.

"A village near, its Moslem ruler said,
  'We've done all possible; now let us go
Where you'll be comfortable, and warm'd and fed,
  Try to forget all loss and present wo;'
At this, the Yankee Captain raised his eyes—
'Who'll guard these goods, meanwhile, from being a
    prize?'

"'Why Allah save you!'—was the Turk's reply,
  'You needn't fear aught from any of us here,
Your goods, unwatched, are safe, and will be—why?
  No Christian lives 'in a hundred miles of here:' "*
The venerable sat down, suppressed applause
Greeting him, followed by a doleful pause.

At this, and lest he might offend right here,
  Young Eblis sought again the open air,
For he had come to have a wholesome fear,
  Lest plaudits given might cause him trouble there;
Incog', anathematized, as if the air he tainted,
He knew he "wasn't so black as he is painted."

* See Note G.

CHAPTER VI.

A Broadway Procession—Want, and its Avengers—" The Devil to Pay "—The Prince at the Capital—Windmills—The Ins and the Outs—The Statue, its Significance—The Monument.

Following again that boulevard, Broadway,
  He found himself one of a vast procession,
Which, without music, flags, or such display,
  Seem'd of that promenade to have possession;
The saddest sight to the whole earth e'er known,
Which Luna casts her pitying glance upon.

It was the ceaseless flitting of young girls,
  Fair as the fairest, hundreds of them were;
Yet homeless, friendless, reckless midst the whirls
  Of surging life which swept on tireless there:
Faces were there which once might angels grace,
Where but despair had left its deepest trace.

No "Lotos Club" had they the entreé to,
  Although, to them, of all the thousands round,
Should come forgetfulness to veil their wo,
  To hide from them the furthest gulf profound,
Which waits their steps as vanishing from sight—
They seek the shelter of oblivion's night.

Yet on all sides who dared take action here?
  Who termed "respectable," could pity show?
Who lap'd in Fortune's smile had sigh or tear,
  For wo so palpable to each one's view:
How "priests and Levites" all, with hurried stride,
Discreetly "passed by on the other side!"

Yet "God is merciful," the good book says,
  More merciful than man, we fain would add,
And in the trust that "His are not men's ways,"
  The consolation comes for all that's bad:
There is no "shuffling" at His awful bar,
For things not made right here are righted there.

Amidst these changing scenes from day to day,
  Of reckless cost or want which men would hide,
Midst the wild rush for lucre or display,
  A shadowy host moved by on every side:
Fearful, mysterious, on their errands bent,
They were the Avengers on dread missions sent.

From out the thousand subterranean dens,
  Where darkness, dampness and fierce Want lie hidden,
From streets, plague-stricken, poverty in pens,
  Contrast with wealth, each foul disease seem'd bidden:
From lowest haunts they came like vapors creeping,
On Fashion's avenues their appointments keeping.

For when they mounted to the gorgeous place,
  Where prodigal display had made its home,
When fever-smitten Dives must "turn his face,"
  Like prince of old, "to the wall," to meet his doom—
Who could not see the Avenger's presence there,
Proud Luxury brooded o'er by dark Despair.

They were indeed avengers, for when Pride,
  And cold Neglect, and Scorn had done their best,
To build each lazar-house:—and when beside,
  Dire Want, Disease and Death had bred foul Pest,
Why hope to keep such enemy in bound,
Destined as 'twas to prey on all around.

The devil saw "compensation" in this all,*
  That here his sire's investments paid him well;
For when a follower "dwelt in marble hall,"
  Consigning his tenants to an earthly hell,
Such Five Points owner, up town, at his ease,
Forgetting Retribution, forgot Disease.

* See Note H.

All did not see this, but young Eblis did,
  And sometimes felt like mentioning the obligation,
But finally concluded that instead,
  He'd let the Reverend Spikes serve the occasion;
He told them in a very straight sort of way,
"Not mending, there would be the devil to pay."

Of course, to mind this they were not such fools;
  They'd "played it short" so often "on the street,"
That on "long time" 'tweren't much to pawn their souls,
  When this pledge they might not be called to meet;
And so young Eblis yet stroll'd round "on 'Change,"
And of Fifth Avenue still had the range.

The imp got tired of doing the amenities,
  The place was nearer right than he dared hope;
On all sides he had found his sire's affinities,
  And Annexation seem'd now but a joke;
For if there was aught true in the situation,
'Twas annexed already beyond disputation.

Next as a diplomat, with no mark'd rank or station,
  No written credentials from his sire at home,
The Prince must look in on the Capital of the nation,
  Incog', of course, not wanting honors shown
His "house," or "dynasty," though well he knew,
Of partisans or clients there were not a few.

Resolving and Performance going hand in hand,
  He found himself ere long the Capitol viewing,
In presence of the "Wisdom of the Land,"
  Their arms like arms of other windmills going,
As each arraigned the other for venality,
Corruption, extravagance, and all rascality.

To hear them talk, one would suppose, of course,
  The "other side" were naught but harpies, surely,
That every opponent was but a curse
  To the people, who had trusted them too truly;
But "Buncombe," he learned, caused gab upon these matters,
Where Truth and Rhetoric oft came out in tatters.

For, after all, as near as he could con it,
  'Twas a great battle 'twixt the "ins" and "outs;"
Other and minor issues turning on it,
  'Twas sure to leave the losers in the pouts;
The winners, *au contraire*, sleek and happy, guess,
"Nothing is so successful as success."

Outside, he look'd aloft to see a figure
  Posted atop of that majestic dome,
Black! was it really a colossal n-gg-r,
  Its back turned spitefully on its Southern home?
Is Freedom black that as an African she's painted,
Or was Emancipation thus indicated?

THE PRINCE AT THE CAPITAL.

And then to turn her back upon the city,
  Upon that vista once so bright to view,
The *Freedman's Bank!* and so on, more's the pity,
  That sculptor sculptured "better than he knew;"
Alas, for Afric and that statue symbolical,
A reminder something worse than diabolical.

In sauntering round, the devil came on that pile,
  To prove a nation's grateful heart is tender;
A failure vast on which the world might smile,
  Especially when Spread Eagleism "gets on a bender;"
Illustrating only penuriousness most hateful,
It shows indeed "Republics are ungrateful."

Thank Heaven, the Father of his Country doesn't it need,
  To prove his name and deeds immortal here,
The nation needs it though, because whilst greed
  Holds sway complete in the Nation's Capitol near,
The centuries hence may know how true's the adage,
" The father's sour grapes have set the children's teeth on edge."

That was a stumbling measure—'tis confest;
  But then the lesson it bore could not be spared,
And that takes precedence always, for when prest,
  In this true chronicle, if rhyme fares hard,
Reason at least is bound to have her way,
No matter who or what may her gainsay.

CHAPTER VII.

The True "Third Estate"—The Prince a Lobbyist—Overreached —Mushroom Display—Secretary Subsidy's Levee—Jenkins on the same—"Rings," and their Import.

In glancing further, statesmanship to learn,
  He found the "Third Estate" to be the Lobby;
A sharp, unscrupulous corps who watch'd each turn
  For those who'd win the race for their own hobby;
An ass, gold-laden, Macedonia's king
Found, in most cases, to be just the thing.

And though King Philip had no "mails Pacific,—"
  No "railroad subsidies" or "grabs" of treasure,
The way he carried matters was terrific,
  If to corrupt a city was his pleasure;
And yet in stealing towns and States of Greece,
Our "rings" have beaten him in the art—to fleece.

OVERREACHED.

Scotch Tom could beat King Philip and "give odds,"
    The Keystone State could Macedonia "skin!"
For what with "railroad rings" and other "jobs,"
    Where senatorial honors are to win,
The sharpest Greeks that e'er outwitted Persian,
Would for *our* rings but serve as mere diversion.

To one of these the imp was introduced,
    Credited with "influence in a certain quarter;"
His good looks help'd him and his chum produced
    Proof that his tongue could run as smooth as water,
And—to the imp—the "pool" to make him win it,
Asseverated roundly—"there's millions in it!"

The Prince a lobbyist was thus made at once,
    And for the "Wisdom" straightway "spread himself;"
But sad to say, he proved himself a dunce,
    Compared to his confreres in the race for pelf;
They "beat the devil" in all sorts of "makes,"
And wouldn't "divide" when they had won the stakes.

The imp had learned a deal in all this time,
    Was rounding his accomplishments to a turn;
At least he thought so, and cared not a dime
    So that of life in the Metropolis he might learn:
But bothered at last to ken each scurvy trick,
Was driven to doubt his kinship to Old Nick!

He turn'd from these to note the swift career
    Of those who sudden climb to highest places,
And found that scores of those arriving there,
    Came up from the provinces the poorest cases;
Men who their board-bills couldn't liquidate,
In a year or two would be living quite "in State!"

Levees, grand dinners, straight would stun society,
    The cost of which no fellow could unravel;
Palatial grandeur, luxury in variety,
    Would shut the mouths of all who else might cavil;
The cost of flowers alone would be the pay,
Yearly, perhaps, of the lord of this display.

And then, outside, to scan the avenues,
    Were equipages quite royal as they lumber'd,
Of these same lords of display, titled parvenus,
    Their "liveried" contrabands, gold lace encumber'd;
With buttons like pewter dollars, the gorgeous flunkies
Look'd down on all their race like grinning monkeys.

The Devil reflected—Was this sneaking love
    For regal pomp innate in all mankind?
Was nothing here to make men rise above
    The vices of the Old World,—left behind?
Is nothing left for the chiefest but to ape
The puerile follies of each foreign state?*

        * See Note I.

MUSHROOM ARISTOCRACY.

It must be owned, not much; since one idea,
   Which dominates all else, is, that display
Should signalize the entering a career,
   As "public servants" even on small pay;
A wild expenditure made by chiefs of State,
The neediest must try to imitate.

Take an example from one grand "reception,"
   When Fashion's flies buzz round some foolish dame,
Some woman whose small brain has no conception
   Of what should constitute her husband's fame;
Led a wild dance for that stale prize—notoriety,
The rock on which they split, is—"best society!"

The *Daily Claqueur* sends its chief chronicler, Jenkins,
   To dance attendance betimes to get the story;
And what by pumping waiters, nods and winkings,
   Manages to picture it in all its glory;
Exhausting all such terms as "brilliant," "gorgeous,"
What is't but "gush" describing Fashion's orgies!

As how? At Secretary Subsidy's late levee,
   There was a grand display of the best society;
There was Mrs. General Pompanoosuck, with a bevy
   Of beauties richly dressed in vast variety;
Mrs. Subsidy, the lady of the Secretary, shone,
The star in the centre of that glittering zone.

The Misses Ring and Subsidy "assisted;"
　Their graces lent new charms to the occasion;
And every thing that wealth and taste enlisted,
　Made it worthy the Capital of this mighty nation;
Mrs. Secretary's dress was satin, and her diamonds,
Worthy the Queen of one of Sinbad's islands.

The Honorable Mr. Tweedledum was there,
　His noble brow and presence quite a feature;
And Mrs. T. with high "Patrician" air,
　And Doctor Softky the well known "star preacher;"
Other *distingués* shone in perfect crowds,
Whilst belles in laces floated by in clouds.

The Army and the Navy show'd their best—
　The Civil Service wasn't without its quota,—
The Honorables Pinering, Frumenti, *et als*, from the West,
　Shot by in the dance as if from "Keeley's motor;"
The Diplomatic Corps in full attendance—
The whole form'd a *coup d'œil* of rich remembrance.

A few distinguished names he couldn't but note,
　Amongst the foreign element there present:
For one he'd mention Baron Banquerote,
　Of noble bearing and of mien most pleasant;
To study *finance* here, he's taken the notion,
Comparing ours with that across the ocean.

SECRETARY SUBSIDY'S RECEPTION.

Then there was Countess Bonsang, *née* Chiffoniere,
  Here with Count B. of diplomatic fame;
Her queenly beauty drew all eyes upon her,
  Her jewels bore a price beyond all name;
The writer hasn't more than space to glance
At that array which sparkled in the dance.

To give each separate toilette, we despair;
  The dazzling richness haloing each new comer;
The flowers were wondrous, hall and vase and stair
  Were wreathed with roses, making it like summer;
And the grand supper something more than splendid,
Was one that e'en Lucullus might have envied.

So on, *ad nauseam*, from toadying presses,
  Helping the follies they should seek to cure,
Until an insult to the time's distresses
  The people questioned—How much more to endure?
From a Mushroom Aristocracy of "place,"
Which has no parallel with the human race.

The shark has pilot-fish to hunt his prey,
  The lion, his followers, for discarded offal
So each chief plunderer has in his pay,
  Enough of parasites of the genus jackal,
To vaunt his greatness by their howls and cries,
To laud that pomp which all true men despise.

And then what mean these "Rings," this endless
　　plunder,
　What is the *real* significance to all?
It means that *show of luxury*—a wonder,
　Flouting the nation 'till it should appal,
E'en the most reckless, lest there come a day,
When popular wrath sweep all this pomp away.

This plunder means the same as in Old Rome,
　Palaces and villas the fruit of wrongs;
It means at Newport a luxurious home,
　Revels at Long Branch, parasites in throngs;
It means that Wrong to Power has freely pandered,
It means unbounded wealth, dissolutely squandered.

Wealth plunder'd from the people, who on foot
　Have dust from chariot wheels tost in their eyes,
By these unblushing devotees to "loot,"
　Who flaunt their spoils as if to tantalize
The people with successful robbery,
Cheats, political swindles, and other jobbery.

The Aristocracy of Fashion is but poor,
　Trifling, inane, its follies quite untold!
The Aristocracy of Wealth opes wide the door
　For sordid gain to make men slaves to gold;
What is the history of States passed away?
"First FREEDOM, and then LUXURY—then DECAY;"

CHAPTER VIII.

A Trip to the Provinces—Bidding for Souls—A Learned Professor—The Thirst for Glory—The Soldier's Horoscope—The Young Girl—Pride versus Love—The Miser.

The imp, to vary his pursuits somewhat,
  Bethought to make an extra hunt for souls;
He 'gan to believe that these were easily got,
  From what he'd seen so far in his patrols;
To this intent he'd glance the country through,
To see what in this line would come to view.

From time quite immemorial it has been
  The privilege, or prerogative of his sire,
To buy up those he fancied, now and then,
  Giving of gold, or youth, all they desire;
A notable instance was that wondrous "Faust,"
The devil having purchased him at heavy cost.

One object sought in this provincial mission,
    Was some real bargains just in the same line;
Was sure his sire would give him full permission
    To draw *ad libitum*, as from a mine;
And so it promised, despite late revelations,
'Twould prove investment justifying fair quotations.

No need to "bear" the market, since the stock
    Was very large on which to operate;
Although the worst of it was that many mock,
    By their very quality all attempts to "rate;"
Such souls in smallness being infinitesimal,
Trifling as motes that float in space abysmal.

The Prince took various parts upon this tour,
    His role being more than that of mere observer,
Because—as noted—he assumed the power
    To bargain for what he thought might serve a
Purpose to people his realm in full perfection,
With those who leaned somewhat in that direction.

A "learned Professor" was his first device,
    Equipped with glasses and a studious air;
His garb quite clerical, his mien precise,
    His linen faultless, brow just touch'd with care;
His *tout ensemble* of that thoughtful kind,
The world associates with "march of mind."

This wondrous scholar had been in all lands,
  Of Oriental lore was all possest;
He had outwatched the stars on desert sands,
  Of Sultans, Kings and Emperors been the guest;
Had cast the horoscope of each potentate,
Had by his forecast oft outwitted Fate.

And as each mortal—some philosopher says—
  "Is superstitious more than he will own,
Even to himself," it was not many days,
  Till as Astrologer the Prince was known;
And then how often those reputed wise,
Sought by his help to solve life's mysteries.

A youth who came was of that queer profession,
  —For queer it is, when thought upon aright,—
Whose business 'tis to "kill," and his confession
  Was, "Thirst for Glory" in whatever fight;
Could aught be told of that, perchance, red page,
To him yet sealed, of battles he might wage?

"O nothing easier," the devil said,—
  "You shall ride victor o'er an hundred fields,
Shall charge your war-horse over heaps of dead,
  Crush myriad wounded 'neath your cannon wheels;
Friends, comrades, all around you shall go down,
But you, as victor, win a world's renown.

"About your pathway, hurtling shot and shell
   Shall sing shrill lullabies to dreamless sleepers,
And all around shall be the stench of hell,
   As the red harvest falls 'fore Glory's reapers;
Till Silence comes to brood o'er thousands slain,
Where carrion-crows and vultures dot the plain.

"Grief, you shall hear, invoke the unconscious dead,
   Behold vast trenches yawn as earth would fain
Hide in her bosom what the sun should dread
   To look upon on each ensanguined plain;
This carnage all enure to you—anon,
Your soul's the price of Glory such wise won.

"That is in part your destiny—no need
   To make it plainer unless 'tis meet,
Your soul you barter, then you'd best take heed,
   And have your horoscope forecast complete;"
Waving a wand in silence o'er his head,
Upon the wall straightway a picture spread.

An old man, gray and broken, sat alone,
   In gilded chamber rich with trophies rare;
Swords, gifts for valor, medals, jewels shone,
   Thrown carelessly around on couch and chair;
It was the soldier; glory girt his name,
He'd filled to the uttermost the trump of Fame.

THE SOLDIER'S HOROSCOPE.

But where were friends, companions of that youth
    He'd flung away in quest of baubles vain?
Where Love and Hope, and even low-voiced Truth,
    All from his storm vex'd path had fled amain;
"*That* is your horoscope," the devil said,
"Choose! but the consequences be on your own head."

"All right!" the soldier answer'd; he was bought,
    Without expenditure of vulgar gold,
The imp once more surprised as he thought
    Of Heaven's birthright—thus so readily sold;
And next, his visitor was a girl so fair,
That few on earth could with her, charms compare.

She came "for counsel," for before her seemed
    The labyrinth of life, a tangled maze;
Of happiness her bright years through had dreamed,
    But now before her steps spread darksome ways;
Her chaperone and ancient nurse there present,
Could tell how life sped innocently and pleasant.

But now the clouds seem'd gathering o'er her path,
    She was beloved; loved too, alas in vain;
She had incurred her ancient sire's deep wrath,
    Although it rent her heart to give him pain;
But then his purpose was to make her wed
One, she'd as well be allied to the dead!

"Rich and distinguished" he might be—'tis true,
   But what were these when coupled with gray hair?
Was there no way to furnish her some clue,
   From such dark destiny, such black despair?
Must she be sacrificed spite of prayer and tear,
Her heart revolting at a fate so drear?

He'd cast her horoscope, if that such glance,
   Might show what future really was in store,
To reconcile her to that fate perchance,
   She might well shun yet could not all ignore;
Would place before her some one fleeting view,
Some presage of that future she would know.

And so forthwith a silken screen he placed
   Beside him in the suddenly darkened room,
And waving his slight wand, thereon was traced
   The outlines of a picture through the gloom;
Next, golden light stole o'er it like a gleam
Of sunshine in the memory of a dream.

And there before them bloomed a maiden fair,
   Joyous she seem'd as grief she ne'er had known,
Light in her eyes, flowers in her shining hair,
   Whilst brilliant jewels clasp'd her beauteous zone;
As the sweet picture slowly faded out,
What was there shook the girl with fear and doubt?

PRIDE VS. LOVE.

She saw herself, indeed; but saw beside,
  In dim perspective, far off, gray and faint,
An old man standing with her, side by side,
  As if in some cathedral vast and quaint;
Standing beside her 'till her image faded
Out from that scene, as if by twilight shaded.

Her fate foreshadowed, posed for once the devil,
  Ending in counsel to submit to fate,
To heed her sire's wishes lest worse evil
  Befall her should she seem to hesitate;
The next thing seen by Eblis on the street,
Was proof of the dread alliance made complete.

A splendid equipage "in the latest style,"
  Held an old man with that mere baby wife;
Her rosy lips were parted with a smile,
  For Pride had crowded Love from her young life;
The devil exulted—he had won a soul,
For Rank and Riches—what can't these control?*

Then came a palsied, trembling old man,
  In threadbare garb, with staff and wrinkled brow;
Anxious to spin his life to latest span,
  He wish'd to consult the learned Magician now;
He really feared of Want he'd be the prey,
Could divination drive these fears away?

---

* See Note J.

Known for a miser, pitiless in his power
  Of wrenching gold from tenants on every side,
Hoarding life-long, as if each future hour
  Stood for a thousand 'gainst which to provide,
He yet would have his horoscope forecast,
He wish'd to judge the future by the past.

He wished to see himself!—so standing there,
  The learned Magician brought his semblance forth,
And lo! an ass it was, gold-weighted sore,
  Whilst cropping thistles by the side of the path;
The end of the way nigh, soiled and travel worn,
Death stood to unload him of that treasure borne.

THE MISER.

CHAPTER IX.

"Vessels to Honor and Dishonor"—Eblis as an Angler—Fly-Fishing and its Victims—Capture of an "Interviewer"—New Locations for Shooting Galleries.

The Professor next, not to neglect his own,
  Accepted an invitation, nothing loth,
To visit a famous prison, and though prone
  To limited associations with "the cloth,"
He, with the chaplain took his jaunt that day,
To see his outcasts as they'd sing and pray.

In the great corridor the crowd were gathered,
  Some hundreds of fierce men, cowed, silent all,
With downcast looks their very passions tethered,
  Their murderous instincts held in dubious thrall;
How savage eyes occasionally were lighted!
As memories flash'd athwart those minds benighted.

At last the preacher rose to tell the story,
  Of fallen man's deplorable condition;
But that "e'en *they* were ministers to God's glory,
  Despite their crimes, their woes in full fruition;
For why? Whilst some were born only to honor,
Others were created vessels of dishonor." *

What? queried Eblis!—mortals made such wise,
  They must of course be denizens of hell?
What boots my mission if this source supplies
  Souls fitted only 'mongst my kin to dwell;
Men made to suffer living deaths on earth,
Condemned to vengeful passions from their birth?

Created wrong for the benefit of their kind!
  Born to illustrate crime to the bulk of the race,
The woes that wait on passions unrestrained,
  Only that others may such "wisdom" trace,
Such "goodness" worship, such "benevolence" love!
Are these the oracles sent from above?

I'm doubtful on these points, to say the least,—
  —So questioned Eblis with a quiet laugh,—
I don't believe this simple-minded priest,
  Who makes himself a "messenger of wrath;"
If I was one of these caged bits of malformation,
I'd beat such sconce to pieces, "sans hesitation."

---
* See Note K.

Young Eblis next as an Angler tried his hand,
  Casting his lines around on every side,
And wondrous luck he had on many a strand,
  Catching his prey where flowed each human tide;
"A passing swearer with bare hook he baited,
And caught him deftly though at low price rated."

In "fly-fishing" his hooks were mostly veiled
  By brilliant hues to entrap the adventurous kind;
To catch political hacks these seldom failed,
  They'd dash at them as if to danger blind;
"Oaths," "resolutions," "principles"—what were they?
The devil's bright lures entrapping them alway.

These lures would be of almost every sort,—
  To bait a Congressman, show a Foreign Mission;
Whilst smaller fry on all sides could be caught
  By bobbing before them his vacate position;
Indeed, most places above these or below,
Were open to any baits the devil could throw.

A poor "divine" he baited with a mitre,
  And "landed him" although a "heavy catch,"
Without a gaff or net, for he was quite a
  Willing victim to that sort of snatch;
He hooked a briefless lawyer standing by,
By dangling a judgeship 'fore his eager eye.

Sometimes he caught a monster without baiting,
    This was the case when once his line he threw,
And up from a school of "devil fish" in waiting,
    A long starved *gallinipper* came to view!
"In the devil's name," cried Eblis, "what are you?"
"O!" buzzed his prey—"I want an interview!"

"An *Interviewer*, are you?" So he took
    And put him as a "specimen" under glass,
And giving the ogre a dry sponge to suck,
    Sent him to the Smithsonian:—but alas!
They curtly wrote—they wanted no such "whoppers,"
They were plagues quite as common as grasshoppers.

"We know the nature of the creature here,
    With vampires, leeches, gnats and such we lump 'em;
No sooner does his hum strike on the ear,
    Than e'en the greatest *wilt*, and let him pump 'em;
The vampire fans them sleepy so 's to fix 'em,
Whilst the ferocious gallinipper straightway sticks 'em."

Next, in plain terms, the devil was offered a church,
    They must somehow recruit their treasury,
As well as ranks, so as not to be left in the lurch,
    Whilst running 'gainst a rival house near by;
They offered him apartments, at least, I say,
Where, "in cahoot," they hoped the concern would pay.

THE INTERVIEWER.

That English parson who was here of late,
   And came on as a connoisseur in puppies,
Who as a dog-committeeman was first rate,
   Was welcomed as a "lion" by the uppies;
'Twas thought of parading him around to make
The empty sack of the church stand up quite straight.

No longer an institution termed "divine,"
   They'd run it on "strict principles of finance;"
"The days of miracles" were past lang syne,
   And any thing from that source was mere chance;
If sales of pews slack'd, as they would at times,
Must start a "restaurant" to raise the dimes.*

If that too, failed, when choicest "oyster supper,"
   Came from fair hands through the unequalled "kitchen,"
If after all the ladies could do, the upper
   Ten couldn't be coaxed in such a way to pitch in,
Perhaps the attraction of a "Ten Pin Alley"
Might do, if helped by a good "Shooting Gallery."

'Tis true a well intentioned man, "struck dead,"
   For only "putting forth his hand to save the Ark
As it was falling," was remembered,
   But that was back of the "Ages" termed the "Dark;"
The Lord didn't watch his own so closely now,
But left them to get on as they best knew how.

---

* See Note L.

And if old-fashion'd people's hearts were rack'd
   To see the "Sacred Edifice" so used,
They felt a dubious comfort in the fact,
   That 'twasn't really the "Lord's House" so abused;
Because, o'erwhelmed in debt 'twas plain to see,
It really was the house of the mortgagee.

The devil finally consented to deputize
   Some of his followers to help the thing along,
And hoped, in time 'twould be no great surprise,
   To see a lager beer department running strong;
Since there's no telling these enlightened days,
How far the church may approve the devil's ways.

CHAPTER X.

Agrarianism—The Red Flag—Beer or Blood—The Meaning of a "Divide"—The Tramps—"The Man with the Poker"—Earthly Hells.

Next, as the devil sauntered forth one morn,
   There came the sound of music to his ear,
Of drums and trumpets on the soft air borne,
   In fitful strains as closer it drew near;
And then the measured tread of many feet,
As a vast crowd surged through the city's street.

Horsemen and vehicles swept proudly on,
   A motley host with banners flaunted high,
With mottos, emblems, many colored, borne
   Beneath the azure of the summer sky;
Carnage was symbolled in the red flag there,
A thirst for blood born of some wild despair.

"Down with the rich! divide each broad domain!
   Give up your luxuries! divide! divide!
No wealth! no capital! let each refrain
   From garnering gold, or else let wo betide;
Cease plundering the poor more wealth to amass,
Lest 'bread or blood!' be the stern cry at last."

And as each eye dwelt on those waving scrolls,
   More rigid seemed the clutch of armed hand,
More wild each trumpet blast, more fierce the rolls
   Of drums and wheels to startle all the land;
E'en Eblis look'd aghast as on they strode,
At this new phase of man's fierce thirst for blood.

Perhaps mistaken! was his second thought,
   "Stand and deliver!" might be all in all,
Despite these bloody symbols, cheaply bought,
   Despite the mottos on each flaunting scroll;
Had it been "beer or blood" 'twould have been more
   plain—
So mused Prince Eblis with a devil's disdain.

The Prince a political economist was, you see,
   And couldn't make out on that tack how it was
That hundreds of millions of good grain could be
   Turned into drink without a thought or pause,
For consequences so deleterious to the race,
Who thus as bread destroyers caused this waste.

He laugh'd at the joke to thus cry "bread or blood!"
   It should be *beer* or blood, he chuckled again,
And didn't believe when it was understood,
   That thinking men would join in the old refrain;
They might—in other lands—not whilst the West,
Deluged the continent with grain of the best.

To be sure these malcontents did have just cause,
   For cries against monopolies and wrongs,
Against the sharks and sharpers who make laws
   To endow with charter'd rights the favor'd throngs;
Men legislated for as privileged classes,
Those millionaires who rob the helpless masses.

The great procession halting in the shade,
   Prince Eblis following, loiter'd up 'longside,
And singling out of the ranks a jolly blade,
   He sought to learn the meaning of "divide!"
"What would you do, suppose you got your pile?"
Was the imp's query with a devil's wile.

"What would I do?" cried Pat—"why bless your sowl,
   I'd have a glorious spree. I would, avic!
I'd have a blow-out that would make things howl—"
   "And *then*?"—was the next query of young Nick;
"And *then*, is't? Whisht! When all was spent for good,
I'd be right in for *another 'divide!'* I would."

"O! ho!" the devil laugh'd, and then his thumb,
　Sought with a jerk the side of his hawkish beak;
Laugh'd?—he just yelled, as with his head aplomb,
　His fingers gyrated. Then next a meek
Expression stole o'er his phiz, he saw his blunder,
When wrathful scowls assailed him, black as thunder.

Not often was he caught so far askew,
　But then the thing was such a treat, you see,
To his sense of the ridiculous at so new
　A thing in statesmanship, it sent him all aglee;
He sobered down in time to 'scape a lynching
From those who claim'd "free speech," sans any
　　flinching.

The devil's experience wouldn't have been complete,
　Unless he'd joined for awhile the army of "tramps;"
A battered hat, old coat, and all to compete,
　Welcomed him to a platoon of the scamps;
He sallied out from the city one dark night,
To see on what adventures he could alight.

The squad that he had joined was the "Devil's Own,"
　Although they didn't know their senior's scion,
A loose allegiance was theirs far as known,
　Although they sought his course to keep an eye on;
To propitiate him, too, on most occasions,
By robbery, murder, theft with few evasions.

But here, as oft before, young Eblis failed,
   They beat the devil outright in their wild raiding;
Such squalor, wickedness, treachery, he bewailed,
   To himself in silence while in mire deep wading,
That ere a week gone out he cut the pack,
And to the city took his course straight back.

A month and more it took to hide the traces
   Of those transcendent horrors so encountered,
For casting about in memory for places,
   Could think of none in which he'd ever floundered,
So much like hell in all that made life dismal,
Not even that pit regarded as abysmal.

There was one "tramp" amongst them had the "blues;"
   "Blue devils," "horrors," "snakes"—"the man with the poker!"
As sots termed mania-a-potu—'till his shoes
   Were filled with reptiles. Stunning the on-looker,
With eyes wild starting almost from his head,
He seemed a being galvanized from the dead.

Horrors alive! How shrank he from the toils
   Of slimy creatures, serpents crawling o'er him;
How gasp'd as choked in fancy by the coils
   Of reptiles in his very throat who tore him;
The devil anew astonished at the sight,
Fled from the scene out to the shades of night.

He thought it o'er when once more back at leisure,
  Thought of the hells on earth, so many, varied,
Then to himself, owned up in fullest measure,
  The drunkard's hell poor humankind had harried,
Until against his wish he was fain to agree,
It matched his sire's so far as he could see.

Betwixt this and the woes which ceaseless roll
  In the nether world, howe'er let fancy aid it,
The earthly tenement was here on fire—the whole
  A living flame as drunkenness had made it;
The devil concluded that all earthly wo
Was bound in that which drunkards only know.

The "gambling hells," of course, were of "tradition;"
  But seldom aught than murder worse befell
Those who in gambling found their chiefest mission,
  Self-murder, at that, to escape an earthly hell;
Of course 'twas but a trifle when the blow
Fell on the innocent and helpless few.

Sober, these gambling "gentlemen" were in most cases,
  Must have "amusement" from eve to the morn,
And what if bloodshot eyes and other traces,
  Told of the wild, fierce disappointments borne;
What if stark ruin waited on such strife,
All this gave "piquancy" to fleeting life.

The devil look'd in on these as leisure came,
  Watch'd the knit brows of slaves to Greed and
    Chance,
Saw the red gold change hands, saw eyes aflame,
  As the doom'd player gave a parting glance
At the piled coins so deftly whisked away,
Till mutter'd curses gave to wrath full play.

CHAPTER XI.

The Prince at the "Hub"—Some Hub Peculiarities—The Puritans and their Theology—Jack and the Parson—Unity and its Difficulties—"Holding the Fort"—Impudence of an Imp—Taste Exemplified—A Stimulant to Patriotism.

The Prince turned up in Boston shortly after,
   He felt quite curious to see the "Hub"
On which the world turns, either slow or faster,
   As this or that celebrity "boss the job;"
He had a liking for the Puritan breed,
Ever since they ran the world by their own creed.

Because, you see, the world is saved or lost,
   Just as they fix it, for they hold the brakes;
And all that happens elsewhere in the vast
   Creation round is purely for their sakes;
A creed most comfortable for them, of course,
Though "a fly on the cart-wheel of the Universe."

THE PRINCE AT THE HUB.

Then Boston is æsthetic—that all know,
  For Art, for Music, Poetry has been noted;
And it is true that in these she's not slow,
  And as authority is often quoted;
But then Theology is her strong point,
Although sometimes 'tis rather out of joint.

Starting so orthodox in burning witches,
  Pounding up Plymouth Rock to stone the Quakers,
Still running public schools with gags and switches,
  And looking askance still at those folks call'd "Shakers,"
The orthodox have had much other trouble,
In tolerating those who will see double.

Whilst "Puritans" to all the world meanwhile,
  The way their theologic team works is too queer!
Reminding one of that old sailor's style,
  Of ploughing in a glebe, the parson near;
He had two oxen with an old mare *abreast*,
And 'fore his patron he was doing his best.

At last, in "beating to windward" of a hedge,
  Where thorns were plentiful, a tangled path,
They jammed together in a sort of wedge,
  And Jack gave utterance to his pent up wrath;
Shifting his quid from one cheek to the other,
He thus expressed to the parson his dire bother:

"The larboard ox is on the starboard side!
—A cussed blunder that on this rough coast—
The old mare's foul o' the rigging and has jibed,
And they're all going to the devil starn foremost."
And saying this he "up helm" and retreated,
Leaving the parson "up a stump" there seated.

Although my anecdote points to a rough conclusion,
   The present case reverses it one may see;
The devil was visiting them without collusion,
   For to slight Boston he could not agree;
There was the place to learn 'bout every schism,
And all the "'ologies," and every "'ism."

I've treated above of that sad lack of unity,
   Amongst those charged with "rooting out all evil,"
That more than almost any other community,
   They couldn't unite in efforts 'gainst the devil;
Bad weeds would grow in every sort of weather,
Because in ploughing they couldn't pull together.

For such bad ploughing in the vineyard spiritual,
   Such inability to cultivate bad places,
They've at last found remedy tolerably effectual,
   By help of one who wouldn't let 'em "kick in the traces;"
They called upon an expert from the West,
And then that plough was seen to do its best.

HUB THEOLOGY.

The devil found a brisk fight going on,
  Between the Hub and one of his own chiefs;
An ubiquitous fellow, who it seems had won,
  And held a stronghold against all reliefs;
The notorious Mammon, and to him 'twas sport,
Against the other side to "Hold the Fort."

'Twas the "Old South" of which he had possession,
  One of God's temples in the olden days,
Where noble patriarchs, a long procession,
  Had come and gone with song and prayer and praise;
The Shrine of Patriotism,—for that too, revered,
'Twas hard to think of any place more endeared.

It was the gathering place in those far years,
  For thousands loved and honored, long since dead;
'Twas hallowed by the sighs and prayers, the tears,
  Which over hillocks green had oft been shed;
At last—"in the way of Progress," all must see,
The "dead should bury their dead!" 'twas Heaven's decree.

And so that devil's lieutenant kept the place,
  Whilst millionaires were deaf to each appeal,
With no more signs of feeling in each face,
  Than on the leather or cloth in which they deal;
The women—bless them—begging here and there,
Trying all ways from wheedling to prayer.

At last accounts, staunch Mammon "held the fort,"
   He couldn't be routed spite of every rub;
His foes in other cities aid had sought,
   With pleas of "impecuniousness" at the Hub;
The last heard too, the women in tears were sitting,
And trying to raise the funds by constant knitting.

Still Eblis went on rambling, all he'd seen
   In Gotham answering for much seen here;
'Twas true the Gothamites were not so keen,
   They showed their worst and with no sign of fear;
But if the Hub a weakness has in 'ts society,
It is upon that score termed "strict propriety."

A little straight-laced were they in all this,
   They washed their dirty linen close at home;
For if occasionally some scandal 'd hiss,
   They'd smother it, nor out would let it come;
And though they had a Brooklyn case lang syne,
They squelched it as they squelch a vile "long nine."

This 'minds me, they won't let people smoke in the streets,
   At least they wouldn't when last time there I went;
And if the smell of the weed a peeler greets,
   He follows up his nose like hound on scent;
Another proof of refinement so complete,
No city can with it on earth compete.

To make his way in Boston "best society,"
  Young Eblis put on immaculate black in dress;
Straw-colored neck-tie, a staid look of piety,
  Slate-colored kids, plug hat to match all this;
He looked the gentleman from "top to toes,"
Despite his beak—I should have said, his nose.

Query the first—"What was he? Presbyterian?"
  Next—"Had he writ a book?"—all this in whispers,
For, as an English blood, he might if he chose be Arian,
  High church, or low, or be on time at vespers;
But finally, the question with a baker's dozen,
Was—"What is the rent-roll of our English cousin?"

But gold and brass can beat the best Krupp gun,
  In carrying all before them, rightly handled;
Young Eblis lacking neither, soon begun
  On Fashion's lap to be most fondly dandled;
His very beak was voted just the thing,
A proboscis quite fit to grace a King.

And as a ship will sail when she has headway,
  And not without, the devil on various tacks,
Sailed round this island, up that neighboring bay,
  On his new voyage in quest of salient facts;
On these odd explorations warmly bent,
He carefully took soundings as he went.

In Art, he found the best that they could do,
  Was just to raise a monument, so hideous,
That to compare it with aught else to view
  On earth, would to the latter seem invidious;
The money went for it, a fact quite clear,
But where was Taste when ugliness cost so dear?

A lighthouse sans its lantern, wrongly placed;
  A clumsy obelisk travestying the Egyptian;
And then whatever way we see it faced,
  Begirt with rubbish of the worst description,
Placed there to chronicle lang syne defeat,
As a factory-chimney 'twould be hard to beat.

It may be averred that Patriotism led
  In heaping up a pile of stones so high,
As savage tribes or friends of warriors dead,
  Raise tumuli by offerings from each passer-by;
A boulder or a clod thrown on, 'twas gain,
So that the mound rose high above the plain.

But Boston's classic, she reveres the antique,
  The beautiful, the æsthetic, as I have said;
Then where was Trajan's pillar? where the Greek?
  That these did naught for the illustrious dead?
The devil smiled archly as all this he pondered.
"*Die* for thy country? Fool, live for 't"—he maun-
    dered.

A COLLEGE FUNGUS.

CHAPTER XII.

A College Fungus — A "Base" Infliction — Periodical Departures Celestialwards—Clams and Contrition—Celestial Ferry Tickets—Pagan Christianity—Experiences of Job and Moses—Finale.

The imp whilst on his cruise one summer's morn,
   Came on that college fungus, a "Regatta!" *
In which young gentlemen, stripped to the brawn,
   Seek *fitting* honors for their Alma Mater;
Thousands upon the shore agape had gather'd
Ready to bet their pile on Yale or Harvard.

Some talked quite learnedly of those Greek games,
   Which made Athena famous long ago,
Dwelling quite fondly on illustrious names,
   Ending with that famed calf-carrier, Milo;
Whilst some protested in quite savage phrase,
That "colleges were but circuses now-a-days."

        * See Note M.

Here was the "sport," the gambler by profession,
  With jeweled shirt-front, rings on dirty fingers,
Young "limbs of law" whose courts were ne'er in session,
  The shootists, "shooting teams," and "pigeon" wingers;
Here were the hangers-on in trotting races,
The myriad idlers from all ranks and places.

Because, you see, it isn't brains that tell
  In life's great race, as once, to win a name;
It's "arms," or "legs," the handling of a "shell,"
  Or foremost place as "tramp," that gives men fame;
But whilst one tramp may win both fame and gold,*
Ten thousand—cursed—are "left out in the cold."

Here was the school-girl jostled by the roué,
  The innocent school-boy betting his first dime,
Whilst parasols, 'kerchiefs waved in air on high,
  Betrayed impatience with fleet-winged Time;
There the poor student, with wild, eager eyes,
His watch in pawn, hoped yet to win the prize.

Here were sharp journalists inwardly groaning, growling!
  Striving with cheerful looks to hide their sorrow,
Over the stuff to set their printers howling,
  When all this nonsense must be told to-morrow;
Here were the telegraphers who had to pound it
Off on the wires with looks which said—"Confound it!"

*See Note N.

A BASE INFLICTION.

Too well they knew the whole thing was a bore,
  That though the victimized would not "own up,"
That e'en the Great Pestilence hardly plagued 'em more,
Than this eternal swash which would not stop;
The news-transmitters, those imposed on classes,
Talked of an "indignation meeting" of the masses.

Meantime, the Race! "Old Prex" put on a look,
  As if quite proud o' the flock he had to train,
But one could see that dragg'd from learning's nook,
  Like hen with ducklings, the good man was fain,
When thus his brood was bent on taking water,
To *seem* delighted, and just follow after.

At last, the Start! Not quite so bad's the Greeks,
  The lads had shirts and drawers at least upon 'em,
And as they "spread themselves" until their breeks
  Were like to burst, how loud the cheers rang on 'em;
—One belle to another, as the crews came to the tussle,—
"O! dear! *You* Jenny,—note Tom's splendid muscle!"

"How?" queried Eblis—"the boot on 'tother leg?"
"Black Crook" again, despite all Grecian graces!
And if the "Amazonian march" is just a peg
  Above this show of "muscle" in the races,
It's only numbers makes piquant the scene,
 A "distinction without a difference"—I ween.

Let all that go, however—if mere "sport"
  Is college training now, 'twas not of yore,
When the bright years of youth were all too short,
  Of needful learning to lay in a store;
The Prince again was posed to find a college
Teaching aquatics as its chiefest knowledge.

Just on a par with this same College fungus,
  Is that marked nuisance of some thousand noodles,
"Base ball," yclept, which fairly rooted 'mong us,
  First—as was natural—struck the Yankee doodles;
And why?—because if Fashion leads the game,
All Yankeedom must profit by the same.

As how? Because, like numerous things beside,
  Skating, croquet, somebody makes the tools;
And start 'most any thing on Fashion's tide,
  You'll have an army large enough, of fools,
To pay the *sharps* who set the thing in motion,
If but the *flats* should happen to take the notion.

So we have "Red Heads," "Red Shanks," Old Nick knows what,
  "Black Legs" perhaps, pitted 'gainst one another;
And a long list of terms, far best forgot,
  Showing, perchance, how "Black Legs" "Red Heads" bother;
When up town Noodledum has seen these capers,
The last infliction comes in the daily papers.

CLAMS AND CONTRITION.

Of course for these small torments there's no cure,
  They "run their course" like any other disease
That poor humanity is called to endure,
  For sin of Adam, or perhaps of Eve's;
Base ball, at last, has come to be a pest on
The community worse than Sergeant Bates or Weston.

There is no end, howe'er of Fashion's freaks,
  It's fashionable at times, to try for Heaven!
At least to feign of trying it in streaks,
  Dash'd with the smallest bit of worldly leaven;
They've found somehow that on a summer tour,
They can make a long tack for the heavenly shore.

As how? Well, well, it takes some funds to do it,
  A "cottage" at Martha's Vineyard* 's the first condition,
And if so comfortably housed that one don't rue it,
  An overdose of clams may bring contrition;
And when all Fashion's host has gather'd there,
At one huge clam-baking, who need despair?

All know that Sidney Smith—the Reverend—says,
  "A bit of cheese may cast one utterly down;
May cause remorseful pangs in a thousand ways,
  May make one feel as if 'neath Heaven's frown;"
To clams, add blue fish, crabs and all Nantucket,
Who is there wouldn't feel like "kicking the bucket?"

* See Note O.

Ergo! it's just the place to go once in awhile,
    To reckon profit and loss in weal or wo,
And though far off, the world looks on, to smile,
    When Religion and Fashion take the trip in Co.;
The chance outsiders have of coming in,
Would seem to depend on—*whether they have "the tin."*

You see the spot's an island, and your fare
    To that celestial portal must be paid,
Before you can set foot upon it, where
    You have a chance to join the cavalcade,
Who muster there *only when it's very warm*,
Resolved, by themselves, to take high Heaven by storm.

The devil next found some *pagans* in his range,
    —Indeed, our country furnishes not a few,—
Those who were so in love with the "great change"
    That comes to all, they kept it close in view;
And not so much for themselves were they concerned,
It was for the *old*, "their hearts within them burned."

A common sight was some poor aged dame,
    Who'd worn herself out in her children's care,
Who'd poured out on them love beyond all name,
    Through nights of sickness, days of toilsome wear;
But—*"past her usefulness"*—that's the heathen phrase,
They couldn't help grudging her further length of days.

PAGAN CHRISTIANITY.

But who thinks of reverence from youth for age!
    What's love, or gratitude in this, our day,
For those who've borne us through life's earlier stage,
    Watch'd us at times with tearful agony,
As young life flicker'd, spite of love's deep yearning,
As when we watch a feeble taper burning.

And if gray locks have come of all these cares,
    If fading vision, wrinkles, weaken'd forms;
If in life's battle age has won such scars,
    And can no longer bear up 'gainst its storms—
Why!—"past their usefulness," e'en let them go;
The grave a refuge from all further wo.

This is the bitterness of life, at last,
    That all our struggles to new sorrows tend;
That looking backward on Life's chequered past,
    Affection e'en may fail us in the end;
The Age grown selfish, eager, sordid, wise,
Spurns the once loved where gold's the chiefest prize.

One Christian dame wasn't in much haste to leave,
    Despite all said of promised joys above;
Dear, simple soul, she couldn't help but grieve,
    To be thus plainly pushed off even "in love;"
"I suppose, dear sister, you're resigned to die!"
"I s'pose I might as well be"—came reply.

O! how "resigned" all were to the "dispensation,"
  Which by the fireside made a vacant chair,
"How thankful that Grandmamma in her condition,
  Had not the burden of more years to bear!"
The South Sea Islands match'd this, Eblis queried,
Where the old by the young, *alive* were duteously
  buried.*

As Eblis saw all this, he did not wonder
  That Job's experience seem'd a type of all
Created man, so thoroughly a blunder,
  He once was drowned off this terrestrial ball;
That Job, the "patientist" cursed "his birth," as was fit,
The "meekest murdering an Egyptian"—as 'tis writ.

The devil got weary of these scenes, at last,
  Too near a duplicate of his first impressions;
He 'gan to flag instead of going so fast,
  And got impatient, such were his confessions;
And disappearing as suddenly as he came,
Was seen going up Hoosac Tunnel in a flame.

* See Note P.

APPENDIX.

NOTE A—Page 25.

From the Newport Daily News.

* * * * We have over and over again this summer witnessed men and women thus locked in each other's embrace, whirling round the hall, while hundreds gazed upon the scene. * * * * * Would a young woman, or any woman, permit a man to embrace her thus in a private parlor, whom she had only known for a few days, or perhaps just been introduced to? No. Is it any more excusable in a public hall, and where hundreds can witness the indecency? No. It is even worse. If such amorous amusements are to be indulged in public, decency requires that it should be done in the dark! * * * * * * *

"But it [the polka] is worse than vulgar. It is *essentially indelicate*, and should be held in abhorrence by pure-minded American women. Because of its indelicacy Queen Victoria prohibited it at her court, and we would not that the wives and daughters of American citizens should in practical delicacy be a whit behind a European lady and queen. The indelicacy of the dance was an objection almost universally made to it when first imported, both in England and in the United States. The objection continues to exist, though it is less loudly and frequently urged, and the reason therefor suggests painful and alarming thoughts. The sons and daughters of Americans have become familiar with and attached to that which their parents abhorred."—*N. Y. Com. Adv.*

NOTE B—PAGE 26.

One who holds a lady's hand like a "muff"—"*without squeezing it!*"—*Dictionary of Fashion.*

NOTE C—PAGE 29.

The following problem is given by the Rev. W. H. H. Murray, of Boston, for solution by the readers of the *Congregationalist:*

"What right has the Park Street church to take up $600,000 worth of the Lord's property in such a way, that it can give religious opportunities to only 1,500 people in the morning, and 800 or 1,000 in the afternoon; when it might be so invested as to carry the strength and consolation of the gospel to 10,000 or 15,000 people every Sabbath."

THE UNCHURCHED PEOPLE.—At a recent meeting held at Brooklyn to consider the present system of religious administration in its relations to the unchurched masses, Rev. Mr. Martin, agent of the city mission and tract society of Brooklyn, presented a computation of the church-going and the unchurched masses of that city, which showed that, after deducting 124,000 children under ten years of age, who are excused from church attendance, the two classes indicated bear the relation of 4 to 9, or 90,000 church-goers to 367,000 non-church-goers—and this in a total population of 581,000. Rev. Dr. Duryea emphasized Christ's commission to the church to "go" and preach the gospel, and said that "if people will not go to the church the church must go to the people." Rev. Dr. Tyng, Jr., declared that the church had lost her power in proportion as she has departed from the working classes. "*We build churches,*" he said, "*for the aristocracy, and chapels for the snobocracy, but the great shopocracy are left out in the cold.*" * * * * * *—*Springfield Union*, Oct. 25, '78.

NOTE D—PAGE 29.

"A hospital for sin." This term need not be cavilled at, since divines are in the habit of speaking of sin as a "disease;" and if the term "fever hospital," etc., is proper, then no violence is done to the feelings of even the most fastidious by the term first mentioned.

"Whittaker's theory that a physician ought to go to the sick and not to the well, is one not very much in vogue among parsons and churches now-a-days : witness the rank growth of steeples in the well-to-do quarters of cities—mortgaged and bankrupted steeples, too many of them."—*Rev. Edw'd Eggleston, in "Roxy."*

NOTE E—PAGE 34.

"The natives are called Rejangs, and form a distinct nation from the Malays of Menankabau. * * * * Their dance consists of little more than stretching both arms back, until the backs of the hands nearly touched each other, and holding the edge of the scarf between the fingers. This peculiar figure they take *in order to give their busts the fullest appearance possible, and captivate some of the young men looking on*."—*Bickmore's East Indian Archipelago*, page 496.

NOTE F—PAGE 48.

"As an instance of the reverse effects of strikes, may be noticed the introduction of new forms of machinery to take the place of the striking workmen. The late coal strike led to the use of machinery in anthracite 'coal breakers,' and the men and boys employed to separate the coal are permanently thrown out of work. In puddling furnaces strikes have done much to advance mechanical puddling : and in the nail trade the striking nail machine tenders have been replaced by self-feeding machines in a large number of shops."—*Scribner*, Vol. XI., page 301.

NOTE G—PAGE 63.

"I landed over these [boats] and stood on the jetty. I offered the waterman a silver coin, the value of which I did not rightly know ; he shook his head, took a very small coin from his pocket and showed it to me, assuring me that a greater payment was not due to him. *So honest are the Turks;* and every day during my stay there I had fresh proofs of their honesty. *The Turks are the most good-natured and fair-dealing people I have* ever encountered."—*Hans Christian Andersen in Constantinople.*

NOTE H—Page 66.

"The air of our London rooms, says Tyndall, is loaded with this organic dust, nor is the country air free from its pollution. * * * * * * The Professor then goes on to develop a very remarkable theory, which attributes such diseases as cholera, scarlet fever, small pox and the like, to the inhalation of organic *germs* which may form part of the floating particles."—*Routledge.*

NOTE I—Page 76.

"Unfortunate as have been many of Grant's cabinet appointments, there are to-day some ladies in the cabinet [?] who redeem it—ladies of culture and elegance, who are of *patrician birth*, and fair, spotless fame. There is not in the United States *a more queenly woman* than Mrs. ——. Mrs. —— is slightly above medium height, with a commanding presence and *high-bred bearing.*"

"Mrs. —— carries with her a dash of the *old regime;*—she will be welcomed by those who form the *better class* of Washington society."

"Mrs. —— does not possess the *birth*, noble bearing, graciousness nor popularity of the other ladies of the cabinet." [!]

"Mrs. ——'s toilettes are the most beautiful in Washington, her evening dresses being of *regal magnificence.*"

"Mrs. —— displays exquisite taste in dress, all her toilettes being Parisian."—"*Ladies of the Cabinet*"—*Letter from Washington to Philadelphia paper.*

NOTE J—Page 95.

"Commodore C. K. G., aged 70, and Miss L. W. R., of St. Louis, aged 24, were married last week. The groom was a former partner and confrere of Commodore V., and is worth several millions. The bride is pretty, accomplished and wealthy, and the Commodore has known her since childhood."—*Springfield Union*, Oct. 25th, '78.

NOTE K—PAGE 100.

A veritable sermon and application of a text.

NOTE L—PAGE 105.

From the *Interior*, Jan. 3d, '78 [St. Louis column].

"Formerly, amongst Protestants, it was only the poor and feeble churches that resorted to 'fairs and festivals' for the purpose of church revenue. But now, especially in St. Louis, the rich churches are taking advantage of the popular method, and we have had a series of popular 'entertainments' for this and that church, a few going as far as to *advertise the beauty and social standing of the ladies who would wait on the guests.* I supposed the 'PRETTY WAITER GIRL' business had been monopolized by the saloons; but times are changing."

The Rev. Mr. Moody, at Baltimore, thus paid his compliments to "church fairs:"

"And there are your grab-bags—your grab-bags! I tell you there is too much of this. Your fairs and your bazars won't do, and your voting, your casting of ballots for the most popular man, or the most popular woman, just helping along their vanity. I tell you it grieves the spirit; it offends God. They've got so far now that for twenty-five cents young men can come in and kiss the handsomest woman in the room. Think of this! Look at the church lotteries going on in New York. Before God, I would rather preach in any barn, or the most miserable hovel on earth, than within the walls of a church paid for in such a way. What is the use of going to a gambling den when you can have a game of grab with a lady for a partner?"

The words are pertinent, and it is time churches everywhere had put an end to such methods of raising revenues.—*Inter Ocean*, Nov. 12th, '78.

NOTE N—Page 127.

Boston Correspondence Springfield Union.

" To abolish these sports is neither practical nor desirable. But the present fashion of their pursuit [boating and ball playing] is *a positive and great evil.* The strain upon muscle, nerves and brain, the consumption of time and vitality required to get up and carry through a contest like the Worcester race here described with even more than newspaper sensationalism, is *an unanswerable condemnation of the custom if people will be rational."*

(Chicago) *Alliance Correspondence.*

"'Old Yale' seems to be making more effort to educate and cultivate a taste for gambling than for legitimate and honorable pursuits. It costs over $5,000 yearly to maintain the Yale Boat Club, and at each regatta thousands of dollars change hands. Students visit loan offices and pawn their last article of jewelry to get money to bet on a boat race or base ball match. The Yale boat house is located on one of the principal thoroughfares, and from early spring until the close of the term dozens of students are seen rowing in a perfectly nude state, except a slight covering around the hips. If complaint is made to the police of this indecent exposure, no notice is taken of the complaint. Young ladies are forced to run this gauntlet of indecency, and subject to the taunting and insulting remarks of these nude students. Complaint after complaint has been made of these outrages to the authorities of Yale, but to no effect."

NOTE M—Page 128.

This is what the London *World* thinks about the Athenians and walking matches : " Long pedestrian walks are a disgrace to humanity. Athletic sports and a healthy cultivation of the body are excellent things in themselves, but imagine the astonishment of the Athenians—those fanatical worshipers of the beautiful—could they have beheld a worn-out, jaded man, with the hunted look of a wild animal, tramping wretchedly round and round a gloomy inclosure for the edification of an ignorant and gaping crowd, this being the modern English version of the Olympian games."

NOTE O—Page 135.

Bishop Haven, writing from Mexico, and of the convent of *El Desierto*, and its wonderfully beautiful and attractive grounds, famous too, formerly as a resort " for gallants and ladies and citizens from the metropolis to walk and make merry in "—says further:

" *Like Martha's Vineyard*, it had ceased to be so much a spiritual, as a *luxurious* resort. Will the camp meeting to come here [in Mexico] FALL UNDER A LIKE CONDEMNATION ?"

NOTE P—Page 140.

"An old lady has just died in the Buckfield Poorhouse who had two sons, both farmers, in good circumstances."—*Springfield Union*, Sept. 6, '78.

www.ingramcontent.com/pod-product-compliance
Lightning Source LLC
Chambersburg PA
CBHW030347170426
43202CB00010B/1279